HAL•LEONARD
INSTRUMENTAL
PLAY-ALONG

TENOR SAX

SMOOTH JAZZ

ISBN 978-0-634-02771-0

HAL•LEONARD®
CORPORATION

7777 W. BLUEMOUND RD. P.O. BOX 13819 MILWAUKEE, WI 53213

Visit Hal Leonard Online at
www.halleonard.com

MORNING DANCE

CD
- ◆ 1 : With melody cue
- ◆ 2 : Accompaniment only

By JAY BECKENSTEIN

TENOR SAX

BALI RUN

CD
- ◆3 : With melody cue
- ◆4 : Accompaniment only

By LEE RITENOUR
and BOB JAMES

TENOR SAX

Medium fast
Electric pno.

JUST THE TWO OF US

CD

5 : With melody cue

6 : Accompaniment only

Words and Music by RALPH MacDONALD,
WILLIAM SALTER and BILL WITHERS

TENOR SAX

Medium Groove
Keyboard intro

THIS MASQUERADE

CD
- **7**: With melody cue
- **8**: Accompaniment only

Words and Music by
LEON RUSSELL

TENOR SAX

SILHOUETTE

By KENNY G

TENOR SAX

HARLEM NOCTURNE

Music by EARLE HAGEN

CD

11: With melody cue
12: Accompaniment only

TENOR SAX

SONGBIRD

CD

🔷13 : With melody cue
🔷14 : Accompaniment only

By KENNY G

TENOR SAX

BREEZIN'

Words and Music by
BOBBY WOMACK

TENOR SAX

TOURIST IN PARADISE

By RUSS FREEMAN

CD

17 : With melody cue
18 : Accompaniment only

TENOR SAX

15

SHE COULD BE MINE

By DON GRUSIN

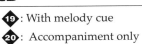

CD

◆ 19 : With melody cue
● 20 : Accompaniment only

TENOR SAX

WE'RE IN THIS LOVE TOGETHER

CD

21 : With melody cue
22 : Accompaniment only

Words and Music by KEITH STEGALL
and ROGER MURRAH

TENOR SAX

rit.